boyzone ... by request

WITHDRAWN
FROM STOCK

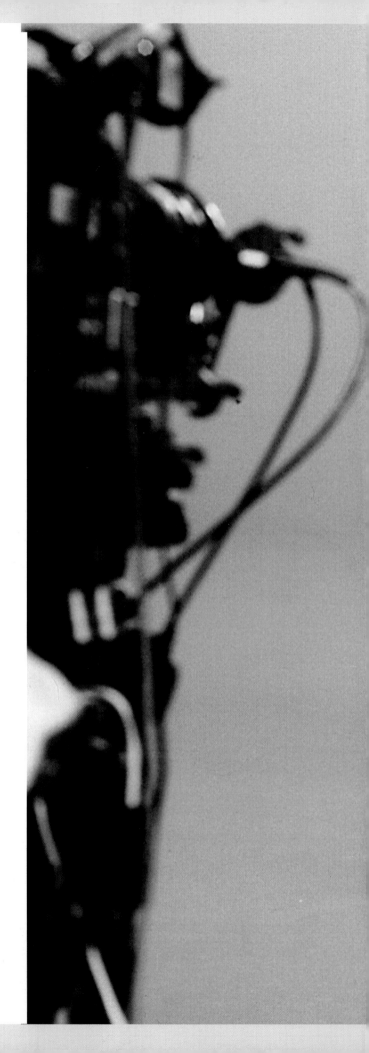

First published 1999 by Boxtree
an imprint of Macmillan Publishers Ltd
25 Eccleston Place London SW1W 9NF
Basingstoke and Oxford

www.macmillan.co.uk

Associated companies throughout the world

ISBN 0 7522 1812 3

Photographic reproduction by Aylesbury Studios Ltd
Printed and bound in the UK by Bath Press

Photography: **BP Fallon:** pages 16,17, 40, 41, 52, 87, 91, 92, 95 main picture, 98 top, 100 top left, top right, 103 main picture, 105, 106/107, 110-113, 115-117, 119; **Sinéad O'Connor:** back inside flap; **Stephen Gately:** back cover, top; **Philip Ollerenshaw/ Idols:** title page, pages 4, 13, 14, 20, 22, 23, 25, 27, 31, 32, 33 bottom left, 34, 35, 38, 39, 95 top right insert, 95 bottom right, 103 bottom right, 120, back cover; **Ray Burminston/CPL:** page 49; **Ray Burminston/Idols:** pages 6/7, 67-69; **Tim Brett:** bottom right, page 100; **Mauro Carrago for Comic Relif:** page 109; **Andy Earle:** cover, inside flap; **Robert Ellis:** pages 71 bottom right,99; **Phil Knott:** page 92 bottom left; **Poppy Lloyd:** page 101; **Allison Maund:** page 100 bottom left; **Nazarin Montag for Comic Relif:** pages 77-79; **Mike Prior:** page 21 bottom left; **Telecine:** pages 8-11, 21 top, 44, 53, 62-65, 71 top five, 73, 80, 81, 83, 85; **Dave Willis/Idols:** pages 37, 55, 56, 58/59; **Steve Wood:** page 45.

This book is inspired by the Boyzone greatest hits album By Request (Polydor Records).

"Everything is the opposite of what it is." - Dr. Winston O'Boogie.

"Reality is a state of mind." - Seth Nettles.

boyzone ...by request

Introduction

WORDS BY
RONAN KEATING, STEPHEN GATELY, KEITH DUFFY, SHANE LYNCH, MIKEY GRAHAM
AND
BONO, DAVID BOWIE, BP FALLON

"OVER THE PAST SIX YEARS WE HAVE PROVED EVERYBODY WRONG, INCLUDING OURSELVES SOMETIMES."
- KEITH

IS IT ROLLING, BOB?
Conversations recorded separately in Ireland, England and Ireland.

BP: All right, who are you?

MIKEY: I am The Emperor.

BP: What do they call you?

MIKEY: Sir (laughs)... O Great One.

BP: What do you do?

MIKEY: You know what I do. Sing. I am a singer/songwriter extraordinaire.

BP: Are you good at it?

MIKEY: Good at what I do? Yeah, I am good at what I do but I don't do what I do all the time. What I do, alone, musically, is different to what I do all the time with Boyzone.

BP: And how would you describe what you do independently of the band?

MIKEY: A lot more variation, a lot more gutsy, a lot more emotion. That's my opinion.

STEPHEN: The weirdest microphone I've ever seen.

BP: Why?

STEPHEN: Looks like one of those Blankety Blank twenty years ago ones. (Sings) "Blankety Blank, Blankety Blank".

BP: (Laughs) Who are you?

STEPHEN: I'm Stephen Gately.

BP: And what do you?

STEPHEN: I'm an entertainer.

BP: Are you any good at it?

STEPHEN: That's not for me to say. I'm alright, yeah. I'm alright at it, yeah, I'm good at it.

BP: Not special, no?

STEPHEN: Yeah, very special, yeah, very special. My mummy told me that as well (laughs).

KEITH: All right, here we go.

BP: Who are you?

KEITH: How'ya doing, I'm Keith Duffy from Boyzone.

BP: And what do you do?

KEITH: Em, I'm one of the lads that make up a successful pop group from Dublin and basically I'm an entertainer and I'm quite good at it.

BP: What do you do, Shanno?

SHANE: I'm a fashion guru, that's what you called me in your last book anyway.

BP: And are you any good at this profession?

SHANE: Absolutely brilliant at this profession. Musically, I'm brilliant. I have to be No.1 all the time.

BP: And you're humble as well?

SHANE: Very humble man, me.

BP: OK, who are you?

RONAN: A policeman wouldn't ask me that! My name is Ronan Keating, born on 3rd March 1977.

BP: What do you do?

RONAN: I've been in a band called Boyzone for the last six years.

BP: And are you good at it?

RONAN: I enjoy it. But there's still a lot to learn to be good at it.

BP: But... people who think you're really brilliant at it, are they wrong?

RONAN: No, if people like it that's fantastic. But there's always someone else that you have to entertain...

BY REQUEST: THE SONGS AND THE VIDEOS

I love
the way
you love me

RONAN: A song Louis and myself wanted to record three years ago. We went to America and I put a vocal down and it just didn't sound good and it was put on the wayside and never listened to again. And then Colin Barlow became our A & R man so Louis and myself said "Listen, we want to record this." The guys liked it, we recorded it, it was a fantastic production. It ended up being a single so it was kinda funny 'cos this song had been around for three years, but nothing ever happened with it before now.

BP: And who's song is it?

RONAN: It's a country and western song from a guy called John Michael Montgomery, kinda Garth Brooksy kinda vibe.The video was shot on location in Glasgow in the middle of our UK tour, our second last one, our tour previous to this one. We didn't have time to go into a studio so we filmed the gig live on stage and also arriving at the airport , in the cars back to the hotel. So that's how it was shot, like a fly-on-the-wall type of thing more than a 'staged' video. It was a lot of fun.

MIKEY: Lovely song, lovely lyrics. I enjoy performing it. The video was done up in Scotland during our last UK tour. It was pretty much fly-on-the-wall type of stuff, y'know.

SHANE: That's the one we did in Glasgow. I was very impressed with the end result of that video. We didn't have much time, it was actually a good video for what it was.

KEITH: I really like the video, it was one of my favourites. It was great. Scotland is a fantastic place to gig. The fans are electric up there. They get on great with Dublin people, they have a lot in common with Irish people. So it was right to do a video up there, it was correct, 'cos we were doin' a live video as well as a bit of other footage and it was just a great, great place to do it. The song itself... I actually really, really like... I really do, I love performing it on stage. The split vocal with Ronan and Stephen is fabulous, I think more of our songs should have been like that all the way through. Stephen's voice has come on in leaps and bounds, as has Ronan's. But Stephen's voice and his personality and his sense of humour and everything about him, I see Stephen as a star, he's definitely star quality. I Love The Way You Love Me, the video was great fun, it wasn't hard work like videos usually are.

STEPHEN: It's a beautiful song and I really enjoyed singing on it and performing it on stage. And the video was really good fun, just kinda what it's like on the road. The nice side of it, I mean it didn't show all the getting up in the morning and being half wrecked, it showed you when you were all fresh and made up and ready to shoot a video. But it showed what it's like,

 all the travelling and being on stage, before you go on stage. It's quite a nice video. The one thing that annoys me about the video is that you see a lot of the girls screaming, and they actually

should have put the screams in on top of the song, to give it an extra feel of being live, and that's what that video misses. But, other than that I was very happy when I seen it... lovely production on it.

BP: Give us a couple of lines of the song.

STEPHEN: Now? Sing it?

BP: Yeah, well talk it then, recite it.

STEPHEN: I'll recite it. "I love the sound of old r'n'b, but you roll your eyes when I'm slightly off key, I like the innocent way that you smile, from soppy old movies you've seen thousands of times... ". There we go.

<u>No matter what</u>

STEPHEN: The rest of the lads would say that that's my baby, that song. It was the biggest selling single for us, it opened a lot of markets for us, a lot of people bought the album because of it. It all started off when I was invited around to Andrew Lloyd Webber's house 'cos I was interested in musicals. And I went around to his house and I sat down and was just chatting away and saying, "I really like musicals, I'd like to do something in the future," and then he says "Oh, let me play some stuff, there's some stuff I'm working on at the moment," and he plays some songs and he plays a demo of No Matter What which was much... slower and much more theatrical. And I heard something in it... it just clicked with me and I said, "It's a really nice song, I like that," and he says, "Would you like to record it?" An honour working with Andrew LLoyd Webber, recording one of his songs. I went into the studio and I recorded it by myself. Then he invited me down, I sang it at this place called Sidmonton, which is a festival that he has where he shows off all work that's coming up in the future. And some of the record company heard it and they liked the song as well. So we sat down to record a new version and get Jim Steinman to produce it and we put Ronan down as well as myself. And what else happened, let me see... The record company... initially wanted to release a different song off the album and we didn't want that song and we says, "No, let's release 'No Matter What'", there was a good feeling about this. And they did and it was number one for weeks and has been number one in a lot of other countries and it's been the song of the year in England last year. So I was very proud. Good A & R man meself (laughs). The video as well was quite nice. We didn't know what to expect. I mean, this big balloon and a big round house type of building... but when I seen the finish I was very happy with it. Very happy. We all looked very smart in it. I was glad I got the opportunity to work with Andrew Lloyd Webber and Jim Steinman and do the song. It was very nice.

KEITH: That's a weird one. Originally that was Stephen's little baby. His Andrew Lloyd Webber song - massive Andrew Lloyd Webber fan, West End fan, plays, musicals - and it wasn't really anything that the rest of us were kind of introduced to, y'know. So basically what happened is Andrew actually asked the band and Stephen to come along and sing No Matter What at his 50th birthday party in the Albert Hall. Ronan did a split vocal on it, helped us, it worked a little bit better to make it into a band song rather than a Stephen song if we were goin' to perform it this particular night. So it went down fantastically and Capital Radio really liked it and start playin' it off the air, started tellin' everybody it was our next single and it wasn't our next single. But the song that the record company had chosen to release was a song that none of the band wanted to release. So we thought it would be a great idea to use the Andrew Lloyd Webber 50th birthday party as a video, so we wouldn't have to shoot a video, and release that as a single. So as it happened Andrew Lloyd Webber was delighted with the fact that we decided to release it as a single and he wanted a proper video made, which was fine. We only had a couple of hours to make the video and initially we were a bit apprehensive.

The video was a hell of a lot better than we all expected. It's actually not bad. But 'No Matter What' is a very special song for Stephen and I think sometimes Stephen kinda feels like he would have liked to sing the full lead vocal himself. But we've won awards for that song all over the world and we've all made sure Stephen has got the awards, because it still is Stephen's little baby, y'know. You were an extra in that video, weren't you? (Both laugh.) Then there was this kind of oriental-looking girl...

BP: And the black guy...

KEITH: And the black guy and the little boy carrying a guitar over his back. But I don't really know the concept behind it. It was just a feel-good kind of video.

RONAN: A strange one, because Steve had been a fan of Webber's and visited him one night at his house, and Webber said he had a few songs there, Sir Andrew Lloyd. And he said he'd love Stephen to sing one. Well, of course Stephen said we would love to, and he took away the tape, picked one of the songs, which was 'No Matter What', and put a vocal on it. And nobody knew exactly what was going to happen with that, but it was done anyway. Then came along his 50th birthday in the Albert Hall...

BP: Stephen's?

RONAN: No, yeah, yeah exactly, Stephen's 50th (laughs along with BP). And we all went along. And while all this was happening the record company were asking what was the next single going to be, and they wanted another song on the album that we didn't want as a single. So we were saying, "No, no no, we don't want that to be the single, we'd rather go with something else." So this 'No Matter What' wasn't even going to be on the album, Stephen was the only one who had a vocal on it. So along comes Andrew Lloyd Webber's 50th in the Albert Hall. Stephen did the vocal, I did the vocal and we sang it at his 50th birthday in the Albert Hall. And the next thing, the buzz about it was incredible, so we said, "Let's compromise, the buzz is fantastic about 'No Matter What', let's put it on the album and release it as a single." The record company were wary of it, but in the end they agreed to it and it became our biggest single to date. It's definitely the song that has opened more doors in more countries for Boyzone than any other record we ever released. So it's weird how things work out, y'know. I'm not going to say we knew better than the record company but it is funny, because we chose that song.

BP: And was it part of 'Whistle Down The Wind' at that point.

RONAN: Yeah, it was always going to be a part of 'Whistle Down The Wind'.

BP: And what about the video at the Roundhouse?

RONAN: Phew, yeah, it was a weird time but I thought it was shot beautifully, actually. The girl on the skis with all the lights was fantastic and then the balloon travelling through the ceiling was... it was a good video actually. We were very surprised at how well it turned out.

BP: How did it feel doing a song by Andrew Lloyd Webber and Jim Steinman? Does it matter really who writes the song?

RONAN: No, it doesn't matter once as it's a great pop song and that's what 'No Matter What' was, a fantastic pop song. We were honoured to work with two guys like that.

MIKEY: Didn't like the song initially. Well, not I didn't like it, that's a bit too strong a word to use, but I wasn't sure about it. Then slowly it grew on me and now I... really like it. Like it a lot. And the video for 'No Matter What' was...?

BP: Roundhouse.

MIKEY: Roundhouse, that's right. White suits and big hot air balloon. Were you there that day?

BP: Yeah.

MIKEY: That video... from looking at what was going on there on the ground, we thought it wasn't going to be a successful looking video at all and it turned out that it was. Turned out looking very very good y'know.

BP: Does it mean anything to do an original song by Lloyd Webber and Jim Steinman or does it matter who writes them?

MIKEY: It means a lot to me because I have the highest respect for Andrew Lloyd Webber and his achievements and his talents and secondly because I'm interested in rock music and Steinman, he'd done all the Meatloaf stuff which I'm a big fan of. So to me it was an honour and a pleasure.

<u>All</u>
<u>that</u>
<u>I need</u>

<u>Baby</u>
<u>can I hold</u>
<u>you tonight</u>

RONAN: All That I Need was something different. It had a very black r'n'b feel to the song, which was something we hadn't really touched on. A lot of people have said my voice was soulful but our music had never wandered down that track, so this was the first song that I felt was r'n'b. I don't mean Otis Redding and Marvin Gaye, I mean the r'n'b that's happening today such as R. Kelly or Babyface or Boyz 2 Men or Brandy.

KEITH: The song I thought was brilliant, it was a step in the right direction for Boyzone at the time. It was a more hip tune to be releasing as a boy band.

STEPHEN: I like performing All That I Need on tour. I always do the harmony up from Ronan so it's quite high but I enjoy it. It's very well presented, very nicely written.
BP: Very nicely wrote.
STEPHEN: Very nicely written, the Dublin coming out in me now! It was a good day makin' the video, a good laugh. We were up on a roof top and it was freezin' and the wind was blowin' and we were in the same building where All Saints made Never Ever.

KEITH: One of my favourite songs to date. I love the Tracy Chapman version but I actually think our version was very, very good as well. I really love it. I think Ronan done a fantastic vocal on it.

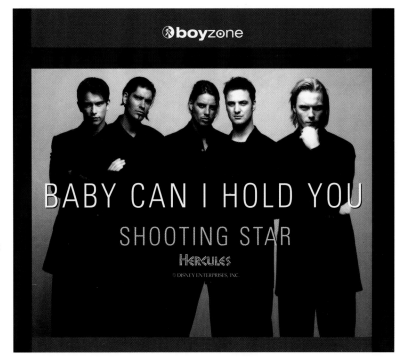

STEPHEN: I love the song, I love the original by Tracy Chapman. Great album, that 'Fast Car'. People kinda said, "Oh not another cover version, what's it gonna sound like?" Ya have to do songs justice when you do a version of them and this one we did. People looked and said "Ah, it's really nice". The video was a fun day. I got the bad deal. I was up earliest and I left last for some reason, which was a pain!. But, it turned out a good video. The only bizarre thing about that video is that although we're in it we're not lipsyncing to any of the backing vocals. It's just the main vocal from Ronan. But that was a good day. I think we done 'Words' in the same studio.

BP: Recite some lines out of it that you like.

STEPHEN: The opening line "Sorry, that's all that you can say", y'know. "Baby, baby can I hold you tonight", just really beautiful lyrics. She's got a very brilliant way with writing. Writing about life and things that just happen everyday. Miss Chapman. Miss Tracy Chapman.

BP: You didn't describe what the video actually was.

STEPHEN: We all had a different room and I had red room, Shane had a blue room, Ronan had a green room... red, green, yellow, blue and something else. Each a different colour. I think the furniture was kinda red and we were just kind of posing around, just lookin' at the camera, tryin' to look good, half decent, which was very tough for me that day. (Laughs) And every other day.

BP: You don't think you look good?

STEPHEN: No, I never did. Never do. See myself as being alright but I don't see myself as... I'm very lucky to be in a band.

BP: Do you think that being in Boyzone gives you pin-up appeal, rather than how you look?

STEPHEN: Probably yeah, yeah definitely, yeah definitely. I mean, when I was a kid growing up I was never looked at as being a really good looking person. My mates kinda got asked out by the chicks and stuff like that. I think I was very quiet when I was a kid as well, so that probably would explain a lot. Mind you, I am still a bit quiet.

BP: And would you change how you look if you could wave a wand?

STEPHEN: I don't know. I don't know what I'd do with meself. Em, people don't say I'm good lookin', people say I'm cute lookin' but not good lookin'. I think that's what people would say.

BP: Do you think you're cute?

STEPHEN: No, I don't know, no. I don't know. I'm very small, small in height, I'm the smallest in the group. I'm 23 years of age and I don't feel 23 years of age and I don't think I look 23, y'know, unless I grow a beard. But when I'm shaving I look younger, I think.

BP: Are you going to grow a beard?

STEPHEN: Yeah, well I've had a couple of days' stubble.

BP: It's hardly Ronnie Drew, though.

STEPHEN: (Laughs). No, I know. Give me a few years before I get to Ronnie's stage!

SHANE: Actually, 'Baby Can I Hold You' was probably one of the ones I was more interested in although we didn't do any BVs in the video, it was mainly Ro's vocal. I was probably more interested in it because it had a bit of a different edge to it, the different rooms. We didn't do it as a group, we did it more as individuals.

BP: That was the sleazy motel type of job, wasn't it?

SHANE: Yeah, sleazy motel one, exactly. And I kinda liked that. It was just that little bit different, it was alright.

BP: I mean the girls were cute, weren't they?

SHANE: They weren't supermodels but I wouldn't disrespect any of the women that were in it.

MIKEY: Loved the song. Love the original. Big fan of Tracy Chapman. We did a very good version of it. Great video. Enjoyable video. Didn't take too long to make. I just enjoyed the intense moodity of it all.

BP: The nudity, did you say?

MIKEY: MOOD.

BP: Oh.

MIKEY: Moodity, is that a word, is it?

BP: It is now.

MIKEY: The intensity of the mood, how about that then?

BP: No, moodity's a good word.

MIKEY: That's what I like about it and the, eh, introduction of the girls in the video as well. I just found it hittin' the nail on the head in regards to y'know certain experiences and relationships y'know.

RONAN: A favourite song of mine. Actually, Louis probably pushed it more than anyone, he's a fan of Tracy Chapman and he wanted us to record it. I love the song, we all do. It's probably one of our favourite songs for playing on the tour bus, Tracy's version. I went along and recorded it with Steve Lipsom and it's still one of my favourite songs to perform live. The video, we worked with Greg Masuak who also directed Words. I like him a lot and some of us like the video and some of us don't. I like it. I don't know why.

BP: Tell us about the video...

RONAN: The video... a sleazy motel was kinda the vibe, fluorescent lights outside with the motel light flashing, and reds and greens and yellows y'know, cheap carpet and dodgy wallpaper. Everyone of us in a separate room with a different look and I had a jacket on which I loved. It was actually a John Rocha jacket but it was fake snakeskin. It was really cool.

Picture
of you

SHANE: Actually quite enjoyed it. Good video, great song. The fact that Mr. Bean was in the video was 100% what made the video, otherwise it would have been us five lads just standing around. The fact that Mr. Bean came in, it was a very enjoyable day more than anything. It passed the hours that are usually borin', kinda made it a bit interestin'. Brilliant song, though, I have to say, everytime I hear the song I do quite enjoy it.

BP: And was Mr. Bean genuinely funny?

SHANE: Yes, a funny, funny man. I haven't met him before, don't know his character, and to see him jest towards the things that you see him do on television is hilarious, it really, really, is. And as a comedian he's brilliant anyway, so I'm a fan. So that was a good day.

MIKEY: Great song. Great video. Very enjoyable. Nice guy, Mr. Bean, he came down participating in the video. Nothing too deep or intense, just a good vibe, fun, summer, up-tempo track.

KEITH: Ah, what a great experience. The video, we laughed and laughed all day long. We performed it with Rowan Atkinson, Mr. Bean and he got into character and it was just brilliant. It was a great song, *Mr. Bean The Disaster Movie* was a great film to be associated with because we're all big Bean fans. We went to the premiere of it in a couple of countries, in Germany and Britain and around the place and we had a great time promoting that single. It was written by Ronan and he got a Ivor Novello, or whatever you call them. And even today when you do "De, de, de, de, de, de" and you hear the song startin' it's a feel-good song, it's "Woah, here we go, party time!" Love the song, love the video, love performing it.

BP: And was Mr. Bean really genuinely funny?

KEITH: An absolute scream. Out of character he's quite shy, reserved, very well educated, quite serious but shy and, nice, genuinely nice guy. In character he's just a mad man, fantastic. Very professional. Seriously professional.

STEPHEN: We were on tour and we had to take a day off for the video and I remember there was photographers takin' pictures, trying to snap pictures up of us walkin' in and out because we had these Mr. Bean outfits on, the same outfits that he wears. Rowan Atkinson attended, he came down and had a laugh. He came down for three hours to record. A very nice guy, very, very intelligent, very clever. Likes his cars, got a beautiful MacLaren F1, which is, like, a really, really nice car. One day Mikey hit Ronan in the face by accident and Ronan's nose was bleedin' and like literally twenty minutes later our press officer got a phonecall saying "Why are Mikey and Ronan fighting, why have they been fighting?" by one of the papers. Like, they go for it so fast! The song itself was a song I wanted to be involved with but, I didn't get involved for some reason. I was snubbed out of the studio by the producers for some reason, I don't know why. I don't really want to work with those producers, but anyway I'm not going to mouth them off. They done a really good job on the production and I think it was a turnover point for us. People seen us in a different light because it was for the movie *Mr. Bean*.

BP: What lines do you like out of that?

STEPHEN: There's one line, "Didn't you think that I would make a mistake" and Ronan would sing "Didn't you think I would make you a steak", which was quite funny on stage.

RONAN: Mr. Bean, genius, fantastic video, I had a lot of fun. It was our first real up-tempo song that did anything for us, so all round it's a favourite of mine, a favourite song, favourite video. I received an Ivor Novello for that song, so I think I can always look back and easily say that was one of my favourite songs.

BP: What was Mr. Bean like?

RONAN: Fantastic. Genius, great guy to work with, very professional. I'd love to work with him again.

boyzone | Picture Of You

Isn't it a wonder

SHANE: Actually, again another good video, because it was probably the first video we made outside of England or Ireland. Interesting trip, goin' to Australia, private plane, middle of nowhere in the desert, an amazing experience. It's just that bit different, innit? I got to drive the Cadillac. I love driving, so that was again a good two days for me.

BP: And the song?

SHANE: Quite a good song.

MIKEY: Good song again. Good video. I really enjoyed making that video. That was probably one of the most interesting videos that we did, 'cos it was on location out in the Australian outback, a place called Broken Hill, an old mining town. Just all the experience of that video was wonderful y'know, intense heat, some horse riding. Seeing kangaroos, like, at five o'clock in the morning as we were travelling to the location on a dusky highway. Beautiful experience that video. Beautiful experience.

BP: Didn't you have a weird vibe in the plane getting there?

MIKEY: Yeah, em, just that there was a problem or failure with one of the engines, so the pilot brought the plane down 'cos he was concerned about it. That was it.

BP: Were you freaked?

MIKEY: No, didn't care. You go when your time is ready and there is no use in being afraid and no use worrying about it. If it's gonna happen it'll happen, and hopefully it'll happen quick. That's one of the better ways I can think of when it's my turn to go. Bang. Better to burn out than to fade away.

KEITH: What a great buzz makin' the video. Out in the desert in the middle of Australia, in Broken Hill where they shot *Mad Max* and *Priscilla Queen Of The Desert*. I drove the Harley across the desert, man. Very, very well-written song.

RONAN: I wrote it and it was a big step for me. There's actually a line in it which should make more sense to me now, more than ever. (Sings) "Mmmm, isn't it a wonder mmm, mmm, mmm, When you hear a newborn baby cry". It's a song about the wonders and the miracles that happen every day that we kinda take for granted. It was probably our favourite video as a band. Keith was on a Harley and we were in a big black Cadillac travelling through the desert, wind in our hair...

BP: You had some vibe in the aeroplane getting there.

RONAN: Yeah, the engines failed and we had an emergency landing in the desert.

BP: Was it scary?

RONAN: We were all so vibed up and it was such a cool thing that we survived... But when you think about it now it is scary...

STEPHEN: A very uplifting song for me. Myself and Shane usually share the microphone singing harmonies and it's a really happy song for me. The video, it was so hot out there and there were so many flies around, really tons of flies. They had to spend three hours, four hours, longer, editing the flies out of the video.

BP: Why, what's wrong with flies?

STEPHEN: Well, you can't have flies on your video, can you, on the lens and stuff? Nothing wrong with flies. There was this kangaroo. I called Ronan, "Ronan, come here, you have to get a picture of this kangaroo, it's really nice" and all of a sudden it was like "Weeeough", it just scratched Ronan's shoulder to bits. I mean, this kangaroo was so sweet for me...

A different beat

boyzone | a different beat

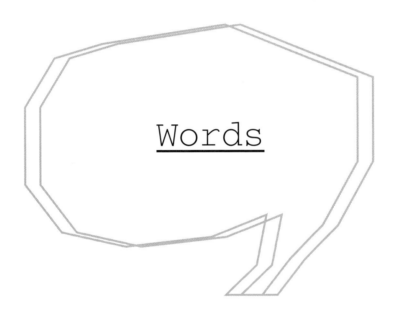

Words

SHANE: Not my most favourite video.

BP: Explain the concept.

SHANE: The one with the rain, that's all I can really remember about it, other than I have a couple of fish that performed in the video as well.

BP: Oh, what happened?

SHANE: Ah, they had a fish tank in the video and I took the fish home and I still have them to this day. Other than that, there's not much to remember about that video, the rain and the fish.

STEPHEN: A song from the Bee Gees, very famous song, nicely written. After the success of it, the Bee Gees, on TV, said it was the best version of any of their songs that anyone has ever covered, which is nice coming from the Bee Gees, who are huge stars. We got to perform it on *An Audience with the Bee Gees* with them, which is a really nice feelin', being up on stage singin' 'Words' with them. They're just so talented. The video was a good laugh. There was a fish tank there and Shane wanted some fish. The lighting was really beautiful and I think we all looked really well in it. I was happy with the way I looked, which is unusual for me. The first time that the five of us sit down to watch the video we never notice each other, we just notice ourselves. Initially the first time you ever see a video you concentrate on how you look.

MIKEY: We done a very good version of the Bee Gees song, and again a very intense video. Quite emotional video, with everybody dancin' away and next they all stand still, with the water just coming down. And it gave that feelin' of ... I don't know whether it's when you're at your lowest point or whatever, but a point in your life when you're not quite sure where to turn next, y'know. That's what I feel from that video anyway.

BP: What would be your favourite Bee Gees song?

MIKEY: I'm a huge fan. The 'New York Mining Disaster', that's a lovely song, 'I've Got To Get A Message To You', y'know, the falsetto hits of *Saturday Night Fever*, y'know, 'Tragedy' and, ah, the whole lot of them.

RONAN: I remember being in Belfast on a tour and Louis arrived with a Bee Gees CD and he says "Listen to track..." whatever it was and it was Words and we all listened to it and loved it so we went into the studio and recorded it with Phil and Ian - they worked on a lot of the East 17 stuff. We did the show *An Audience With The Bee Gees* and we performed that song with them, but before we came on stage Barry turned around and said, "Well, the question from the audience was how do you feel about other bands covering your songs?" And Barry's answer was "Well, you know we have had a lot of bands covering our songs, from Elvis Presley to whoever da da da, and easily the best version of a song was Boyzone and 'Words'" and with that we walked on and sang the song with them. To even **recognise** us is an incredible honour and I also got the fantastic opportunity of singing with the guys in the RDS on stage, 'Words', that was a stepping stone in Boyzone's career.

The video actually was a very interesting video. It was Greg Masuak who did 'Baby Can I Hold You' and it was one of the videos the five of us agree on as one of our favourite videos. Very cool, very calm, it was a kinda café we were sitting around in. Nice vibe.

KEITH: Our first number one. Great song to cover. I'm not sayin' we were better than the original but we were as good as it. And Barry Gibb said that himself so I'm not bein' rude by sayin' that. The video was fantastic, a moody video set in a cafe. It poured with rain in the cafe and we all got soaked. I mean, it looked good on the video. At the time it didn't feel that good, cos the water was freezin'! We were all after been workin' all day and the last thing ya wanted was to be drowned, y'know. We got drowned twice and we had to stay in the wet clothes till we got drowned again. But it was good, very good fun.

Father and son

MIKEY: Good video, hard t'make, lots of black soot and smoke around the place. The song was pretty good too but I hated that dance routine. We all did. It was a nightmare.

SHANE: Something we tried to bring into Boyzone, an up-tempo vibe. We wrote it in Ireland in a little studio in Temple Bar. I do quite enjoy the video. We did it in the old power plant in Dublin and everytime we came out of there, our noses were just full of black 'cos there was loads of fires going on. Good at that time, yeah.

RONAN: The video was different, it was shot down at the Pigeon House in Dublin and there was fire and explosions in it. Very interesting at the time but when you look back at it now it's "What was that?" (laughs).

STEPHEN: I remember sittin' down writin' the song and it was grand, y'know. The video was hilarious. You'd go home that night and you'd be coughing up black and you'd blow your nose and it would be all just millions of black soot comin' out of your nose.

BP: How does it go, give us the jizz of it?

KEITH: (sings) "We're gonna be so good, like ya knew I would, like you know you should, come on and hear me now. Gonna be so good."(both laugh). First video with a dance routine. At one stage I was so depressed about me not bein' able to dance that I thought I was actually gonna have to leave the band. I went home to me Dad and I said, "Listen Dad, I can't dance, there's other people in the band that do things better than me in every area, they're better singers, better songwriters". I said, "I don't think this is my calling, I think I'm out of place here," and me Dad says to me, "Don't be so stupid son, that band needs a whole lot of different combinations of things to make it work, some are in the public eye like the singin' and dancin' and some of them are in the background, maybe in the humour, keepin' people's spirits high". Words of wisdom from me father.

DANCING IN THE MOONLIGHT

STEPHEN: I used to teach dancin' out in Donnycarney, near the North Wall, for under-privileged children, children round the area. I mean, I was one meself. It was just really good fun, really nice to do.

BP: And what do you think about Boyzone as dancers?

STEPHEN: They're all alright, we can get by. I still enjoy dancin'. I like it.

Coming home now

STEPHEN: I love this song. I love the video. I was involved with the writing of this as well, wrote it about being away and comin' back to Ireland. And we shot the video in Dublin.

BP: Give us a line out of that one.

STEPHEN: "I'm coming home now, been so long now, gonna get there somehow, praying you'll be there, shoo be do ba ba". (laughs)

KEITH: My first solo piece in Boyzone. I did a kind of a rap on this song.

BP: Can you remember the rap?

KEITH: It was "Dear the close ones I remember seeing, You're in my heart and overseas, I feel you close and not so far, Soon we'll be together, This time it's forever" (laughs). I wrote that myself, you know what I mean? (laughs).

BP: What is the first line of your song Where Have You Been?

KEITH: The first line? (sings) "You cut the lawn when there was only dirt, You took a bet and lost my shirt" (both laugh). It's funny, I got Ronan to do the backing vocals on that song, reverse the tables for a few minutes!

MIKEY: I'll tell you, there was one very interesting part to that day. We were doing a clip down by the Custom House and I met a bum, a guy who was homeless. And he was a very, very nice guy, a drunk. I was very captured by what he had to say. He used to be somebody, a Major or a General in the army. He said there were times when he used to go to fancy parties, had lots of money and there he was now with nothing. No wife, no, no children, no nothing, just the clothes on his back. And the alcohol. Interesting.

SHANE: I really like the video. We had a bit more attitude, a bit more in your face, walking down a Dublin street, all in black. Loved the song. That actual song was the song we performed for charity at The Point Depot when I met my wife Easther. That was when me and Easther clicked. We knew there was an attraction.

BP: Was it you that flashed your bum that night?

SHANE: Yeah, got me kit off (laughs).

BP: Did she see that?

SHANE: No, Eternal performed before we did. So they'd already left. But she's seen it now in real life! (laughs)

RONAN: It's about a guy who has been away from a girl that he loved and he is coming home to her, but you can look at it any way. Anyone who emigrates, it's a song for them too. It was shot in Dublin down at the Custom House. There's a street down in Ringsend that it was shot on too that a lot of people have used. The Spice Girls have actually used it for 'Stop', one of their singles, so we were there first, girls! (laughs). We met this guy and he was drinking and he was an older gentleman and he was looking at us and going "Ah, you guys are great, I was somebody once". Maybe he was happy there doing that, but if he was saying "I was somebody once" then he can't be that happy. So it made me appreciate who I am and what I have, y'know.

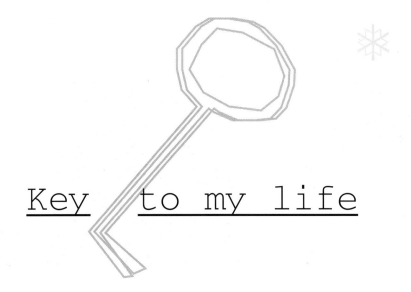

Key to my life

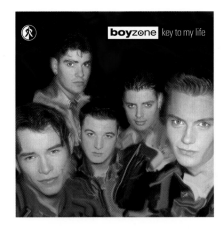

SHANE: Actually an interesting video. We acted a little bit in the video, this school and all that. The song, not such a bad song. I would cringe if I ever thought I would do it again, but on the day it was good.

STEPHEN: Good video, Laura Bermingham, an Irish model in the video, directed by Bill Hughes. I liked it because there was a little bit of actin'. I had to pretend that I was a little school kid who fell in love with the teacher and had to pretend to be really innocent, which I am (laughs). She was a very beautiful girl and very nice to work with. It was set in, I don't know what year, 1920s.

BP: 20s, 30s.

STEPHEN: Yeah, 20s, 30s around that time. The clothes were quite old and the hats, y'know. And Ronan Keating looks really funny in that video. It was just a laugh.

BP: Why did he look funny?

STEPHEN: Just the way he wore his cap. I wore mine backwards and he wore his frontways and he just looks like, em, just looks like a complete farmer, very funny. The song's lovely. We done two versions. We done an up-tempo one, a 12" dance mix which we perform sometimes and we done a ballad and one funny thing is that I always get my cues wrong. I'd be in too early or too late and the lads would be just crackin' up laughing, lookin' at me gettin' the cue wrong but it was a good laugh. Nice song though.

RONAN: Another ballad. It was actually the first self-penned song by Boyzone because it was 'Love Me For A Reason' previous and 'Working My Way Back To You', so it was almost seen as half credible to release this one. We wanted it because it was our own. Listenin' back to it now, it wasn't much of a song but it was important to us then, so you can't really knock it. The video was turn of the century schoolhouse, Stephen was in love with the teacher, we all wore funny clothes and it was shot in sepia. Different.

KEITH: It's funny, we didn't perform this song too much. There was a dance mix made of this song that was brilliant, really, really hip at the time, played in all the clubs and nightclubs around the country so when we went into concert we used to use it as a fast song rather than as a ballad, because it was a ballad. We used to do the disco version of it and just run around the stage like lunatics, bopping our heads up and down! (laughs). The video was fabulous, Bill Hughes directed it. It was shot in an old church in Sandymount and they redid the church into a classroom and they dressed us like the 20s and 30s, you know, braces and ties and stuff like that, and hats on, and we were sitting a classroom and our teacher was beautiful, she was a model. We all had to act, it was great fun. And Stephen had a crush on the teacher and he was writing notes to Ronan or Ronan was writing notes to him and the teacher found the note and found out that Stephen had a crush on her. And Stephen was the outcast of the group in the

class and at break time we're outside and Stephen is off reciting poetry on his own while we're all off having a laugh and getting into trouble! I just have really great memories from that time.

MIKEY: The first song penned by Boyzone, em, myself, Stephen and Ronan over in London with Ray Hedges. Still, it wasn't a bad song I suppose, it was a typical type of pop song. Interesting video as well, again which was in Sandymount. We seem to make all our videos in Dublin, y'know. There was a bit of acting to be done within the video, and

we had this model, she had the part of a teacher, she... good looking girl now, y'know, nice. I actually like that video. There's a nice character about it or something.

BP: Describe the vid. again

MIKEY: Huh?

BP: Describe it.

MIKEY: Well, it's like a school scene y'know we're all schoolboys an' you got this lovely schoolteacher an' Stephen is mad about her like, y'know. And we're all taking the mickey out of him about it like, y'know. An', em, it's good.

Love me for a reason

STEPHEN: Breakthrough. It was just a very exciting time for us. We were starting out as a group, we didn't know what we were doing, we were just breaking into the UK market and it, it was our first single, went to number two at Christmas time. It was just very special to have recorded that song, myself and Ronan done the vocals. Basically it was the song that launched our careers, launched us into Europe and the Far East. Everybody loved it.

BP: Give us a couple of lines.

STEPHEN: "What I'm saying is kisses and caresses are only minor tests babe, Of lovely distresses between a woman and a man." There you go. The video for that was very simple, shot in the POD nightclub in Dublin. John Reynolds our co-manager owns the place. We used lots of candles and there's some really nice jumpers by a woman called Lainey Keogh, who lent us the outfits. I think she was starting off herself and everything went quite well.

BP: And did you like the Osmonds?

STEPHEN: I liked some of the Osmonds' songs yeah, I had heard Love Me for a Reason beforehand, I think it was 1974 was it?

BP: Something like that.

STEPHEN: Yeah, well, wasn't even born! (laughs)

SHANE: The song that entered Boyzone into, I wouldn't say world domination, into worldwide success. It sold very well considering it was our first single. Christmas number two for our first single was a pretty good impact on the music industry and we were dead chuffed. The song, female orientated, a bit in touch with our feminine side if you want to say that. We didn't understand the music industry, we didn't know what way we were meant to be or what way we weren't.

BP: But even visually I mean you had these very camp.....

SHANE: Camp yeah, big collars, big cuffs yeah, very camp,

BP: And then the kind of knitted T-shirts....

SHANE: Yeah, but we didn't understand, hadn't a clue! We should have just done what we always wanted to do and we would have had a bit more cred earlier in our career but ah, you can't knock it. Absolutely can't knock it. It is good to look back on things like that, as embarrassing as they are, many people have embarrassing stories to tell about their early life.

KEITH: We hadn't got an iota what we were doing. Great video for the time, shot in the POD. We were wearing jumpers in the video, Lainey Keogh jumpers, and we felt they were a little bit camp for us and we weren't all that happy with wearing them. But at the time we just done what we were told, it's quite funny to look back on, the little skinny faces on us and the baldy faces as well 'cause we weren't shaving at that stage! Back when we were in good shape and we had small waists! It was good fun. Louis was always fantastic at thinking up songs.

RONAN: This is the one that opened all the doors for Boyzone in the rest of the world. Louis picked it. Louis has a fantastic talent for music and ear that I have never seen with anybody else. Love me for a reason was a song we used to listen to on the bus when we were doing our tour around Ireland in the nightclubs. There's a funny statistic that at one stage in the early days in Ireland for like 38 weeks of the year we were number one, Wow!

MIKEY: Good version of an old song. Good video at the time. It was all shiny and sparkly and young boys and glamoured up and innocent and pure and all look about it y'know. That was the key to the door really, wasn't it?

BP: And were you an Osmonds fan?

MIKEY: I remember the Osmonds. I remember the Bay City Rollers an' all.

BP: Did you have the gear?

MIKEY: Bay City Roller socks an' all! I was only a very young kid so my ma used to dress me up in the tartan, send me out on the street like an eejit for everybody to say "Ahhh, Janey, look at him, isn't he lovely!".

"What do you call five mates

who step into the breach

when you've blown it

with your missus?

...MANZONE"

-Bono

Sweetest thing

KEITH: Louis was talkin' to Bono and the lads in the band and just said the boys would love a song from ya to do themselves and Bono sent over... 'Sweetest Thing'. And Ronan went into the studio and put a guide vocal down on it and the A&R people decided it was the wrong sound for the album that was bein' released at the time. So we said to the lads, "Listen, thanks very very much, but it's not fittin' in with the rest of the stuff that we've already recorded", so they went ahead and recorded it themselves and released it as a single. I remember one day Ronan comin' over to me and sayin', "U2 want me in their next video", and I went, as much as I was delighted for him, I was gutted a bit, 'cos U2 were my heroes and I was goin', "Really man, that's fantastic, brilliant, but I'd love to do that man". So I suppose I went behind the door a little bit about it and I rang Louis up and I just said, "Listen Louis the rest of the boys would all love to be in U2's video". And he says, "They'll probably take three of you". I think Ronan was under the impression the likes of Jack Nicholson and all was in it and I was goin', "No way Ro, I'd love to be in U2's video, man, I don't care who else is in it, I'd love to be in that video!" So as I said I went behind the door a little bit about it and rang Louis and

said, "Louis is there any chance I can get into that video too?" And Louis said, "Well they actually asked for all the band but I didn't think you'd be into it." And I says to Louis, "U2 are huge heroes of mine, I'd love to be in it", and he says, "They actually asked for all of you, I just didn't think you'd want to do it". He said maybe they'll take three of you, maybe you, Ronan and Stephen. So I was delighted with myself. It wasn't fair on Shane or Mikey, but it was such a major thing for me that I was a little bit selfish. I knew Shane didn't care about the U2 music, it's not his type of thing. But Mikey was always prone to sing an auld U2 song from time to time, so I knew he would be another guy that would like to be in a U2 song. So we said... to Shane and Mikey, "Listen we're gonna do this U2 video, we didn't really think that you'd want to do it" And Mikey was, "Aahh I'd love to do that, man". And Shane said, "No way, man, I'd love to do that, man, I'd love to be in a U2 video, that'd be cool". So as it happened every single member of the band was ecstatic about being in a U2 video. So I rang Louis back and I said, "Listen, everybody in the band is ecstatic about bein' in the video, Louis you're gonna have to get us all in there." So Louis rang and they were over the moon that the five of us were gonna do it, so we flew back to Dublin. I've never seen sun shinin' in Dublin as hard and as strong as it did that day, 'cos we were doin' it on the street. It was just such an honour and a pleasure to be associated, for U2 to even **recognise** us. That was enough. That was enough. And throughout the day we came more and more on personal terms, rather than speaking to them as **kings**. They kinda became **people** and we had really good conversations. And we even start jokin' and slaggin' each other, y'know. I remember sayin' to Bono, "It's funny, isn't it , Bono, that U2 had to ask Boyzone to be in a video to get some credibility!" (Both laugh.) Bono just laughed. It was really, really light humoured. And when we weren't recording the four of the U2 boys and us guys were all in the same room, just chillin' out away from the general public and it felt good, it really did. A real inspiration, that day was. Fantastic.

MIKEY: U2, I didn't get to speak much with Adam or the Edge but spent a bit of time talking to Bono and a bit more with Larry. Very impressed with how down to earth they are and nice, just to get on with. After the success that they've had, to be still, y'know, be able to maintain the common touch, that's something that I admire very much of somebody. It wasn't just a good opportunity. It was a personal thing, to be there, to be asked, to be seen with the lads in the same video, that they seen us worthy. It was a good day. I enjoyed it.

SHANE: Doing the U2 video, as a person I now realise it was very, very important - or more so a great experience. I'm not a big fan of U2. I do respect them. I was more into my reggae. U2 weren't such a big part of my life, not as much as some of the other lads are concerned. So I just didn't have the same vibe that they did until now, but we all have to go through those experiences, to realise what was special in life. And I do realise that that was a very special thing to do. I'm a very proud man to say that I did a video with U2.

RONAN: We were actually given the record, probably a year previous, to record it for the *Where We Belong* album. It didn't work out. I would have loved to do it, because it would have been such a fantastic angle, y'know "Bono wrote this song", y'know. How cool. It was a B-side previous but in turn, it's funny how things work out, they re-recorded the song, released it as a single for their Greatest Hits package and asked us to be in the video. It was an honour, it was incredible. In most of our eyes U2 are the greatest thing since sliced bread. And the way they respected us was just incredible. What a fantastic bunch of lads. We didn't have to do a whole load, not really. Just pop up our heads and go, "Ooooh, oooh, oooh, the sweetest thing" and pop 'em back down again. It was fun. Different. Nice.

STEPHEN: A good day, a good laugh. Nice to hang out with Bono and the lads. Nice people, very friendly. Good fun day for all of us, just chillin' out, walkin' up and down the streets. I like doin' open video shoots where people can see you, and people all queuing and lookin' - y'know, "That's Boyzone!" or "It's U2!" I like that, the attention. U2, they're just so talented and such a brilliant group.

BP: And was it funny, Boyzone being in a Uee video?

STEPHEN: Very funny. Actually, the funniest thing in the whole video, I cracked up laughin', is when I looked at the horse and cart that Bono was in - he's goin' by and you can just see my head poppin' up and goin' back down, and then it pops up again. It's funny just to see Stephen lookin' up, **dyin'** to get into the camera! **Missin'** his cue! (both laugh).

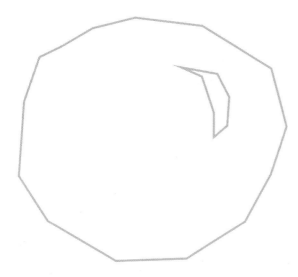

When the going gets tough

KEITH: What a great tune! You know "When the going gets tough, the tough get going", when you listen to the lyrics you can relate it to a charity such as Comic Relief and that's why it suited the song. To record a song like that for our own personal selves I wouldn't have been too fond of it, although I love the song. But for the reasons it was recorded I was 100% behind it. It wasn't a step backwards for Boyzone it was a step to the side to help out somebody else and that's exactly what we did. It was number one for two weeks, three weeks, I don't know, I was away. At the Brits we had three of the best boxers in the world doing backing vocals - Barry McGuigan, Nigel Benn and Chris Eubank. Priceless! And we were all there dressed in gangster suits, with the white ties and the spats and everything and we're doing this boxing routine on stage and it was naff but it looked great. For the Comic Relief situation that was in it, it was brilliant.

MIKEY: Original by Billy Ocean, from the film 'The Jewel On The Nile' made in 1984, Diane Keaton, Michael Douglas, Danny DeVito. They were actually in the original video as well with Billy Ocean. Good bit of craic for a good purpose, Comic Relief. You got to be able to help out.

SHANE: A Billy Ocean song. Billy Ocean, he was good in his day. Great song. It was for Comic Relief and it was a good laugh makin' the video.

STEPHEN: It was good making the video, it was very quick. Actually there was a funny incident where we were all messin', like "What do you want to do in the video?" and they were all saying "I'll do this" and "I'll do that" and I says "I'll do knitting" as in nothing, you know. I was just laughing at myself and they all laughed with me, and next of all I was going down to shoot the video and they showed the treatment and it says "Stephen will be sitting knitting". They took me seriously, like they said "He wants to knit!" and I says "I don't want to knit, you know". So they said "What do you want to do?" So I said "I'll be a DJ instead". So I was a DJ throwing records about. And lots of comedians came down, people from Coronation Street, Graham Norton who done Father Ted, he was in it. It worked well with the charity itself as in, you know "When the going gets tough the tough get going", you know as in a real "Come on let's get together to raise money for a charity". Straight in at No.1 for two weeks. Very proud, very pleased and I loved it.

BP: It's the biggest selling Comic Relief record ever, even more than The Spice Girls..

STEPHEN: Is it? Really?

BP: Yeah.

STEPHEN: Wow, that's good. And a lady who I think didn't get any recognition for what she done was Alison Moyet, she done the B-side, and nobody ever noticed. I really like Alison Moyet and I thought she deserved a little bit of credit for it.

RONAN: When the going gets tough, the tough get locked! We were asked to sing it for Comic Relief and we were honoured and we had a lot of fun. We worked with Kevin Godley, who did the Sweetest Thing video and he also directed my solo video. Lovely guy, good friend. We had a lot of comedians in and different actors and asked them to perform in the video. It was cool. Billy Ocean actually came down to the video cos he sang the original. Said he liked our version. Cool guy, nice fella.

You needed me

STEPHEN: I love this song, it's a beautiful, beautiful song and initially it was supposed to be myself and Ronan who were singing on it. The video is really, really nice. I think people are going to really really like this song and I think maybe it's going to be a big single for us. It's another cover, I know...

BP: Ann Murray, isn't it?

STEPHEN: Ann Murray, yeah. It's a really good song to launch the *By Request Greatest Hits*. People will probably say "Ah, how many covers are on the album now?" There's a really beautiful vocal on it and I'm not blaming anybody but I just wish I had been on it with Ronan, it would have been nice.

MIKEY: One of my favourite songs. My mother used to sing it as I was growing up and she sings it beautiful, so that song to me is precious. Ronan does a lovely job of the lead vocal.

BP: And what about the vid, Mikey?

MIKEY: I thought it was suitable for the song. It's like when somebody is at a point in their life when they go, "Look, I've been a fool" and somebody is there to pick you up. There's a lovely feeling of abyss about the video y'know.

BP: Feeling of?

MIKEY: Abyss. It's like a lost... kinda out there, on your own, different planet type of feeling, y'know.

BP: Give us a line out of it if you like.

MIKEY: (Sings) "I cried a tear, You wiped it dry, I was confused, You cleared my mind... " I'll do the rest in concert for you.

RONAN: A beautiful, beautiful song, another choice of Louis'. I love it, it's one of my favourite love songs of all time. It's what every man or woman would love to say or write about the person they love.

BP: Give us a quote then.

RONAN: My favourite is "I sold my soul, you bought it back for me and held me up and gave me dignity, somehow you needed me". Another one that really strikes me, that I love very much, is the second last verse, "You even called me friend", what a fantastic thing to say. How we take things like that for granted but really they are special. It's beautiful.

KEITH: Our new single. Kevin Godley directed this video and he also did the Comic Relief song and 'Sweetest Thing'. It was an open warehouse with all different picture frames all hangin' at different levels in this big warehouse out in Bray, Ardmore Studios, like in an art gallery but there was no art, was only frames. And the way Kevin was recording it really looked brilliant. It's everybody's own interpretation of what they want to make it.

SHANE: A beautiful song. I do really, really like that song. And it deserves to do well.

All the time in the
world

I never not need you

STEPHEN: 'All The Time In The World', I love it. I'm really happy with it. 'I Never Not Need You', that's a nice song, a good fun song.

RONAN: Keith and Stephen, myself, Lisa and Yvonne went to New York and we had a lot of fun recording, working with Mark Hudson who is working with Ringo Starr at the moment. From there we all went on to Vegas where Keith got married. So it was a fun time...

KEITH: Myself, Ronan and Stephen put down the initial vocals. We finished in Manhattan, flew to Vegas and I got married. They are great songs (laughs).

Was there five minutes that changed your whole life?

MIKEY: If there was five minutes I think they'd have five names, and that will be Shane, Stephen, Ronan, Keith and meself, y'know. That will be the five minutes.

KEITH: No. There definitely wasn't five minutes that changed my life because when Boyzone first got together... well, you're broke and you don't know where you're goin', whether this band is goin' to be successful, whether it's gonna flop, whether it's all a load of rubbish. We scoured the country from one end to the other doin' gigs. Some nights only 8 people turning up, 12 people turning up. Other nights turning up and there's nobody there to perform in front of, so we would have to get back in the van and go home.

SHANE: The five minutes of deciding whether you are going to watch TV or go out with your mates. Deciding to watch *Smash Hits* TV show and seeing Will Smith inspired me into getting into the music industry. And through that I met my wife Easther and even through music I now race for Ford Motor Sports.

STEPHEN: Was it all of five minutes? That split second I suppose, with the 'yes' that I got when I was in the group officially. I didn't know what I was letting myself in for, but that changed my life. Dramatically.

RONAN: Well, it was more like five seconds! When Louis Walsh told me I was in the band, ever since then my life has changed, dramatically.

Has it ever been lonely?

MIKEY: Yes doctor, it is lonely (laughs). At times, yeah. At times it's been lonely and frustrating, confusing, all of that.

STEPHEN: No, never lonely, always somebody around you, always somebody to talk to, always somebody who recognises you, who would want to talk to you. Any time I get on my own, I love. It's more relaxing chilling out, so I don't get lonely at all.

KEITH: I've been with Lisa through Boyzone. She has been my backbone. Lisa has just been there, through thick and thin. She always stuck by me when I don't know why she just didn't run off and leave me. I don't want my life without Lisa. She's very important to me, she is. And my son Jordon is the apple of my eye.

BP: Until you met Yvonne and got married, was it sometimes very lonely?
RONAN: Very lonely, yeah. You find yourself going out weekends when you didn't even really want to go out, you just want to go home to bed and find someone to hold you and tell you that everything is going to be okay. Luckily I found somebody to hold me. And I've got Jack now, too.

BP: Before you met and married Easther, being a member of this mega successful group Boyzone, was it lonely or was it like, a mad rampage?
SHANE: It certainly wasn't lonely. Without sounding soppy, the band had each other - we almost didn't have time for love and romance.

Oh solo me-o

KEITH: If someone left Boyzone it wouldn't be Boyzone anymore. For me Boyzone means five people. The five people that made it, the five people that made it work. At the start it was put on a tray for us, but it wasn't put on a tray that it was successful, we made it successful ourselves. Boyzone is successful because of the members that are in it and nobody knows different.

MIKEY: There is no need for Boyzone to ever break up as such, officially. We can do our own things under the umbrella of Boyzone and above the safety net of Boyzone. I think that would be a more clever idea, rather than officially saying "That's the end, da de da... "
BP: How would you like it to be?
MIKEY: Genesis, that's the kind of idea I think would be best for Boyzone. You can grow as individuals and then when you come back together you have also strengthened the Boyzone thing immensely, y'know.

KEITH: If Boyzone breaks up I guarantee you that every day of my life, every thing I do, every way I turn my hand to do something different, there'll always be a memory of at least one of them, I reckon for the rest of my life. I could never turn my back on the memories of Boyzone, I could never turn my back on any of the members. We've been through so much heartache, we've lain in beds millions of miles from home and cried our eyes out in front of each other, laughed, joked, had good fun, experienced amazing things together. I was the kind of person who wouldn't go on a roller coaster ride on my own because I'd have to have somebody to talk to about it later on and that's what Boyzone was, it was four other fellas to experience it all with. A part of my heart belongs to each and every one of the members. And if Ronan is successful in his solo career and Stephen is successful in a solo career, I'll turn up one day when they're singing on stage and I'll be in the pit and I'll wave up and I guarantee you there'll be tears on both sides. And that's the way it is, y'know.

STEPHEN: It's a choice that we will make when we want to go solo. Ronan's got a single out, I've got, y'know, a single comin' out as well. It's from a movie called *Monkey's Tale*, which will be out around June. Then I'll have a single out during the end of the year, 'Bright Eyes' from *Watership Down*.
BP: You're doing the rabbit's voice, aren't you?
STEPHEN: Yeah, I'm doin' a bunny rabbit's voice. I was a special guest.

BP: So have you thought about the solo situation?

STEPHEN: I want to have a solo album, definitely want a solo deal.

BP: And what would happen if someone left Boyzone?

STEPHEN: I think we'd end it. If someone really wanted to leave, it wouldn't be the same. Boyzone is the five of us. To carry on would be very hard. If somebody wanted to leave and they made that decision, then I have to respect that decision. It's something that they have to deal with and do.

BP: And you wouldn't feel it was a waste of Boyzone, as it were?

STEPHEN: No. This is our sixth year and most bands don't last for four years, three years. Our sixth year, and it's stronger, stronger than ever, so I think it would be fine.

BP: 'Cos you did a solo thing before, didn't you, 'Shooting Star'? Even though it came out under Boyzone it was solo Stephen really, wasn't it? Was that odd?

STEPHEN: No, it was good to do. It was one of my dreams to sing for Disney, to perform a song on a Disney film. It was for Hercules and it was No. 2 in the charts. So that was good.

Shooting star

Snips of Internet chat between David Bowie & Ronan Keating 30/1/99

Do you think Boyzone is the Irish Take That or the male version of Spice Girls?

RONAN: We were more than just a boy band, we wrote our own songs, we created our own destiny in the music industry - especially after 13 Top 3 singles and 3 No. 1 albums. Good question.

DAVID BOWIE: I, on the other hand started off as a Girl Band and slowly became who I am today.

DAVID BOWIE: Do you have brothers and sisters?

RONAN: Three brothers and one sister. My brother Ciaran is your biggest fan.

DAVID BOWIE: How tall is he exactly?

DAVID BOWIE: Who makes the creative decisions as a band? Is it a band thing or is it a management thing?

RONAN: The five of us will usually make a lot of the decisions and decide what's in store for our future, then someone in the record company usually changes it!

DAVID BOWIE: How do you feel about MP3?

RONAN: I think it's a fantastic achievement for our generation, but I think there will always be the need for record stores and record companies.

DAVID BOWIE: Why are you such a bearer of bad news!

RONAN: David - do you golf?

DAVID BOWIE: I had one once, but the door fell off.

DAVID BOWIE: Do you feel a Celtic connection or do you not find that part of you life?

RONAN: No, I'm very proud of where I come from and I'm very interested in the history of Ireland. It's a wonderful, mystical country.

DAVID BOWIE: I feel much the same about Bromley.

DAVID BOWIE: As you yourself write so prolifically, are you thinking of siphoning some of those songs into an album of your own?

RONAN: I have written a song for the new *Notting Hill* project, which is the follow up film to *Four Weddings and a Funeral*. It's called 'When You Say Nothing At All'.

DAVID BOWIE: Do you knock around with Bono or any of U2?

RONAN: I know Bono and Larry, but I'm a terrible name dropper.

DAVID BOWIE: Drop some famous ones then.

RONAN: Elvis, Roy Orbison...

Perfect day

STEPHEN: That was a fun experience. The video, Elton John was in it, everybody, you know there were so many different artists and it's a really beautiful song. I loved that song straight away, heard it long before the *Trainspotting* thing. I just think it was a nice opportunity for us, we were the only pop group to be in it and it was all opera or rock or people who are well liked within the business. It was a great honour to be asked, like the same as the U2 video was a great honour. 'Perfect Day' went to number one as well, for weeks. In the video they wrapped us up in black tinfoil, I don't know why....

BP: Oven ready.

STEPHEN: Oven ready yeah, Chicken A La Ding!

BP: Chicken A La Ding?

STEPHEN: Yeah. Put chicken in the oven and wait till it goes ding! (Both laugh.) Bono was in it too. All proceeds went to the Children In Need charity. I think a lot of people started seeing us in a different light after that video.

BP: And did you know of Lou Reed before?

STEPHEN: Yeah, I've heard of him.

BP: Had you heard of the Velvet Underground?

STEPHEN: What?

BP: Have you heard of the Velvet Underground?

STEPHEN: No, I haven't heard that one.

MIKEY: Great honour. We were the only pop band asked to do it. We've been involved with some incredible stuff, y'know. Good names there, excellent Lou Reed song.

BP: Who did you like who was in the video?

MIKEY: Obviously Bono, Pavarotti... Bowie was in it wasn't he? Em, it's hard to remember at the moment.

BP: Dr. John, Shane MacGowan...

MIKEY: Shane MacGowan yeah. I think he's a genius. Very good lyrically. Some may say if he didn't have such a fondness for the drink he'd have been a great man, but then again if he didn't have a fondness for the drink, it wouldn't open up the genius skills within him. Who's to know? Maybe he'd be nothing without the drink. At least he's something with it.

KEITH: The first time I kinda felt really proud was the 'Perfect Day' video. It was the first time that real pop stars recognised Boyzone. I just couldn't believe I was associating myself with these type of people, like U2 and M People and all these old great singers. They were probably delighted to have us but we never saw ourselves as anybody special. It was just a great honour to do Perfect Day.

SHANE: Not such a big deal for me. It was very special because of all the other artists.

BP: The song, did it mean anything to you?

SHANE: No, it didn't.

BP: And did Lou Reed mean anything to you?

SHANE: No, not the damnest thing. I'd heard the name Lou Reed in passing maybe once or twice but no, not really. But due respect to him.

RONAN: It's a compliment being in the video, when you look at the artists that were there, from Bono to... to everyone (laughs). Man, where do you start?

BP: And did you know Lou Reed?

RONAN: No, I never met him.

BP: No, I mean his work and stuff.

RONAN: Oh yes absolutely, yeah, fan of that stuff, love all that.

BP: Any Lou Reed songs that you like in particular?

RONAN: 'Perfect Day' was actually one of my favourites of his. It came out on the *Trainspotting* album previous, so that brought the whole thing back to me again. What other songs do I like of Lou's... name a few, Beeps.

BP: 'Wagon Wheel'.

RONAN: Nah.

BP: Uh, 'Waiting for the Man', Velvet Underground.

RONAN: Velvet Underground, yeah.

BP: Ahm...ahm, I've gone blank.

BP: You're good mates with Robbie Williams, aren't you?

KEITH: Robbie and me have been good pals, so as you say, Robbie is a friend. I get on with him and have a couple of drinks with him and have a chat, but he's not someone I'd go to when I was in trouble or lookin' for advice, because he's hit the elbow of a lot of hurricanes in this business and been spun. I think he's enough things to sort out himself without listening to my problems as well.

BP: How does it feel now that B*witched are doing so well?

SHANE: It's amazing. Now I understand how my mother and father felt when I started. It's really strange looking at my sisters on the TV. It's a good feeling to see them do so well.

KEITH: I done one night's work once as a male stripper. I was about 18. I was in good shape, training very, very hard in the gym at the time. A couple of blokes came in looking for young-faced, good-bodied blokes. It wasn't an ongoing thing, just a once-off. We never trained, we never rehearsed, we never choreographed. We went there, went out wearing different outfits, took off a few bits and pieces, left the G-strings on, danced in front of about a hundred ladies, had a bit of a laugh. I never told my mam and dad at the time that I did it because they would have been very upset with me.

BP: Were you any good at it?

KEITH: Aah, I wasn't bad. Got a lot of claps and cheers, got £50 for 15 minutes' work. I thought I was loaded! (Laughs). Couldn't believe it.

BP: And why did you seize that rose?

STEPHEN: Seize the road?

BP: Should we go somewhere quieter where we can concentrate better?

Working my way back to you

MIKEY: Not the greatest song in the world but a lot of special memories as life was good at that time. It was a lot more less complicated at that time. Got complicated for a while and then became uncomplicated again. A lovely time for me.

BP: This was the very beginning?

MIKEY: Yeah.

BP: And was it better then than now?

MIKEY: It was different then than now. It was young and innocent and not too sure of life in general, y'know what I mean? I was in love with a girl and thought it was forever.

SHANE: Again, Ireland only, thank God. (Laughs.) Again, I would say in touch with our feminine side, but that's what boy bands were, that's what the vibe was. And we couldn't really get any input from anyone else, because there was no other boy bands or boy orientated pop things musically in Ireland. There was just us lads trying to do it and we hadn't a clue.

BP: And did people think you were complete losers?

SHANE: Complete! People thought we were complete lunatics more than anything (laughs). Thought eh, what are we trying to do in life, like "Cop on lads, it's not gonna work", and I do agree. If I saw a band now doing the same thing I'd be like "Get a life", I really would. But we were only young.

STEPHEN: Oh God, it was grand, it was fine, it was funny. Nice video. We wore no tops in a section of it and were dancin' in a section of it. Myself and Mikey done the vocal, Ronan didn't even do a vocal. And then a while ago they asked us to do it for France, asked to record a French version with a group called Alliage, which I did not want to do. But it's a song we put up ourselves and charted ourselves and done it all ourselves. We didn't know what to do at the start and the styling for that was hilarious. We done it on the *Late Late Show* and afterwards people said "Oh my, here's a group, I don't think they'll last very long!" (Laughs.) People were just sayin' "One Hit Wonders, they'll never make it big" but then we showed 'em! (Laughs again.)

RONAN: George Michael actually said this on *Parkinson*, but it's funny 'cos I went through the same thing. We performed the song on TV and I went into town the next day and I was walking through town looking at people, saying "Hey, do you recognise me, hey, do you remember me?" (Laughs.) It's kinda sad! Nobody knew who I was. It was like anyone who watched turned off when Boyzone came on, and went to make the tea!

KEITH: We had to it a few years later in France with a French band, Alliage. It was actually quite good fun performing it with them. Our video was terrible. At the end of the video you see us all running around like kids and Stephen jumping up into Ronan's arms and Ronan looks about twelve (laughs). Stephen was a fantastic dancer in those days, did a lot of disco dancing, won a lot of championships, Shane was always a great dancer. Me, Mikey and Ronan never had much experience with dancin'. Ronan and Mikey were a lot more agile than I was, I was into the auld body-building before the band. Mikey done kick-boxing for years, I mean the guy can still do the splits now as far as I know!

When you say nothing at all

RONAN: Phew! My first solo single! Daunting, but a special feeling. It's for the new movie '*Notting Hill*', with Julia Roberts and Hugh Grant. I'm looking forward to it. It's really frightening, really scary, because it's my first solo single. It's my move, it's another stepping stone, another chapter. Beautiful song. I don't know what's going to happen with it, I don't know how big it's going to be or how small it's going to be. All I can do is work hard and hopefully it's successful. I've got a good chance because it is on the soundtrack to a big movie. The video, done by my friend Kevin Godley, is me sitting on a bench in a park in Notting Hill Gate, the same bench that's in the movie, with people coming along and sitting down with captions under me, kinda like the REM video for Everybody Hurts.

BP: Are you nervous about it?

RONAN: Yeah, I'm very nervous. But I'm excited about it and that's why I like it.

STEPHEN: Very nice. I like it a lot. I hope Ro does well with it. I'd be very nervous but he's well liked by a big audience.

BP: You'd be nervous that it did well or that it didn't do well?

STEPHEN: Nervous that it didn't do well.

BP: Would you be nervous that it led to a solo situation?

STEPHEN: No, no, no, not at all. If that's what Ronan wants, it's his choice. I mean, I want to do some solo stuff as well in the future. I hope it goes well for him, I really do, he deserves it. He works hard and yeah, I'm sure it will do well. Fingers crossed.

What's left for Boyzone to conquer?

SHANE: A hell of a lot. We are still only a pebble on the beach. Yeah, we've had success, we've had some great songs, No.1 albums, but when you look out there and you look at such artists as Stevie Wonder to U2, to Elvis and the Jacksons, they're the real stars. There is always that status and that level of professionalism to achieve. It's far too early for any of us to think of leaving.

BP: Is it?

SHANE: Most definitely. For example, Gary Barlow, he thought he was on a winner, the next George Michael, and he didn't do a thing, did he? If someone was going to leave Boyzone, they need to think what they're leaving behind cos they're going into the bewilderness, you know (laughs). You're looking into space on that one, to be quite honest. That's just how I feel.

BP: Alright, Mr. Lynch.

SHANE: Alright?

BP: Cool.

SHANE: Sorted.

KEITH: This is called By Request because the reason we're here is our fans have gone out and supported us, and bought our singles and our albums, and by doing that it's them requesting us to stay together to make more music for them to listen to. We do appreciate everything they do for us and we hope that we're giving back enough in return for what they've given us. And to our fans, thank you very very much.

BP: Mr. Duster, thank **you** very much.

KEITH: And Mr. BP, **you** too.

BP: Fair play to you, Keith.

STEPHEN: To the fans for respecting me, for respecting my privacy, thanks very much. To my family, thank you very much. To my loved ones, thank you very much. To everybody in the world who was ever nice to me, thank you. And if anyone is interested in reading a book I recommend 'Conversations With God' by Neil Donald Walsh.

BP: Did Annette Tallon give you that?

STEPHEN: No, I gave it to Annette as a present.

BP: Peace and happiness, Steve.

STEPHEN: Yeah, peace and happiness, Beep.

Is this beyond your wildest dreams or is it your wildest dream?

RONAN: Oh, I love this. I dreamed about this when I was younger. Every night I used to dream about being on stage and performing and singing and just travelling the world and being a pop star. And being a pop - I don't know about the star!

STEPHEN: I've no idea. I don't see it as a dream. I just see it as something that's happening and I'm still goin' along with it, on a long journey, a bus journey and I haven't stopped off. This is not my stop yet. I'm still travellin' and still goin' on, so I see it as a journey more than a dream.

MIKEY: Well, I never expected any of it and I am very fortunate that I am where I am in life. Yeah, I'm amazed at it all but, in order to cope with it so that me brain doesn't explode, I just use the excuse that there is somebody else mappin' the way for me and this is what they must have meant for me.

KEITH: Nowadays I've got bigger and better dreams. I don't mean bigger and better than Boyzone but the dream I have lived in the past 6 years definitely has been a roller coaster ride, a white knuckle roller coaster ride and it's been fantastic. I'd like to be in a movie one day but it's not something that I would go crazy trying to do. If it happens that I do a TV show, presenting a TV show, fantastic. If it so happens that I write my own album well that's something I'll try as well.

SHANE: I suppose it is my wildest dream. Music isn't my passion. I do enjoy it and I'm very lucky to do it, but all the other members of the band revolve their life around it. But I choose to do music as a job, my way of living and to get places in life. It's getting me the establishment that I need to get into motor racing, really.

El Presidente

BP: Where will you be in ten years time?

RONAN: Who knows? I'm lucky to be here now! (laughs)

BP: You're already on the Millennium Committee in Ireland. What about when people say "Ronan Keating for President"?

RONAN: Yeah, go for it man! (both laugh) I'd love to be in that house for a while (both laugh). Who knows? Listen, I said it jokingly one day, said "If Dana can do it, so can I!" (both laugh). And ever since then people have picked up on it and obviously there's some talk about it so .... I don't know.

BP: And would you go for it if you were proposed?

RONAN: If people wanted me to be an ambassador for the country I would accept.

BP: Well you've already been that, haven't you, all you guys?

RONAN: Exactly. So if they want to put me in the house in the Phoenix Park I'll do it, no problem! Nice expense account as well! (both laugh)

BP: And what about the old begrudgers who say "Ah, Boyzone are just silly pop music, da, da, da". What would you say to them?

RONAN: Jealously will get us everywhere! (both laugh). People say "When are you going to change your name? Are you going to call yourselves Menzone?" (both laugh). It's not about that. What about the Beach Boys and the Waterboys and the Beastie Boys? Boys is just another word. Boyzone now is Ronan, Stephen, Shane, Keith and Mikey.

BP: Tell us about being a manager, co-managing Westlife with Louis?

RONAN: Louis found the guys. Three are from Sligo and two are from Dublin. I see in them what Boyzone were five, six years ago. I get involved with their artistic development - how they look, what they sing ...

BP: And what about your solo single vibe?

RONAN: It's something I want to do. I've recorded my *Notting Hill* record and shot the video and it's ready to be released. It's a very exciting time for me. I'm really really nervous. My stomach is in a ball every time I think about it. And if it's successful, well then fair play, if not I can sit back and say at least I tried. And my own music won't be totally different to Boyzone's music. I'm not gonna try and write an indie album, you know. It's still pop music. Hopefully, please God.

Charity begins at home

BP: Let's talk about the charity you've set up and named after your mother, bless her.

RONAN: When Mam died we were all very confused and didn't know which way we were turning. We sat down and talked about it and Linda my sister said "Let's start up a charity" and because of the position I'm in, I could use my name to push that as best I could. Since then it's rocketed. We wanted to set up three mobile units, the Marie Keating Cancer Awareness Fund. We put these units on the road in Ireland to make people aware of cancer, because if cancer is caught in it's early stages it can be cured but if it's too late... We've almost reached our target. Linda has been the one who has really pushed it from day one and fair play to her. And it's our way to, I guess, to deal ... like everyone has different ways way of dealing with losses, it was our way. We don't want someone else to go through what we went through so that's what we did. I believe so much that Mam is with me every second, every step of the way ....

BP: Can you feel her helping you?

RONAN: Yeah, I do. I feel her strength, at times. There's other times I'm lost but most of the time she's there, y'know, and it's wrong cos sometimes I ask too much of her. Like, "Help me here, help me there, help me in this way, help me that way". At the times I need her most she's there.

The kids are alright

BP: And how does it feel being a pop star and a pop?

RONAN: It's pretty cool, Beeps. It's incredible. It's wonderful when I hold him in my arms and he's falling asleep and it's like "This is what it's all about, this is life", you know? Every day I think I'm the luckiest man in the world. I know every father probably feels that way about the child they hold in their arms, but I am. I really am the luckiest guy in the world. I've got it all. And you know, Louis Walsh gave it all to me. He really did, he opened the door for me, he gave me this opportunity. I might have met Yvonne somewhere else on a different road but he gave me this band and the life that I lead today. And I'll never forget that and I'm very grateful. And I'll try and pass that on to as many people as I can and try and touch as many people as I can.

BP: How's marriage?

RONAN: Wonderful, magical. If you can find somebody that you want to spend the rest of your life with, well then you have it sussed. Y'know, not everybody can find the person they want to spend the rest of their life with and I have. I'm over the moon. Yvonne has given me a lovely son, she's such a magical, wonderful person. I'm so lucky to find her, I really am, I'm blessed. And I feel Mam gave her to me almost, set it up.

BP: Come back to being Jack's dad. When you saw Keith's son Jordan for instance or Mikey's daughter Hannah, did you ever think that you'd have a kid?

RONAN: Ah yes I always wanted children. I was always a big fan of kids, I went to school with them, you know! (both laugh) I love kids, they're magical.

The Boyzonettes

BP: Give us a little verbal on the three children, on the Boyzonettes.

RONAN: Hannah is a great magical little kid, she really is. She is a very advanced kid, the same age as Jordan, three. She's an unbelievable little kid, like she sings and she chats and she's not at all shy and she'll talk to ya, a very attentive kid. Jordan on the other hand is very shy. He clings onto his mam and dad and he's the most cutest little character in the world. I love him. He's a brilliant little kid. I like all children, love them. They're fantastic and they're the most innocent naive creatures in the world.

BP: That's the beauty of it.

RONAN: That really is the beauty of children. They just look for security from you and hopefully we can give it to them. And as they grow up they become a personality, a person. It's wonderful to watch that and it will be very interesting to watch Hannah, Jordan and my son Jack develope into people.

BP: And what would you say if Jack in years to come was to come to you and Yvonne and say "Look, Mum and Dad, I'd like to go and be in the music game". What would you think?

RONAN: I'd say "Yeah, go for it man, I'll back you all the way". And I'll try and give as much advice as possible. There's only so much I know but I'd never stop any of my children from doing anything they wanted to do. And I'd wish them the best, I'll be there for them every step of the way.

All along the watchtower

BP: What do Boyzone mean to you as a family?

RONAN: It's unbelievable, the relationship the five of us have built up towards each other. I love the guys. They're very important people to me and I don't think they realise that sometimes. But they are, they've been brothers to me for the last six years and I hold them very dear to my heart. We've created our own little world, our own sense of humour. There's times when we don't get on and we argue but still it's like brothers, I truly mean that, I truly do.

BP: You've been a member now of Boyzone for six years - how do you remember it?

RONAN: It was wonderful. It was magical. It made me what I am today and I loved every minute of it. The downs and the ups and arguments and the fun, it's been the most incredible funfair ride. In the beginning, we got a hard time because we were very much called a manufactured band. That was hard for us to deal with.

BP: And how does it feel now that finally you guys do have respect? Like at the Capital Radio awards thing recently, people like Elton John and Suggs from Madness who's a very good songwriter coming up to your table to pay their respects?

RONAN: Three years ago we would never have got that. That's what we've worked for for six years and we've got it now. And I think that's brilliant, that we have that backing and we have those friends in the industry who will help us do whatever we want to do in the future.

BP: Give us a little message on the record, a little message to the other four guys as we look back over these six years.

RONAN: Thank you for those last six years. I'll never forget them. You've been there for me through up and downs, through my doubts and hardship and joy, losing my Mam, gaining Yvonne. Through it all you stood by me, through the difficult times as well as the great times. We've had problems with each other sometimes but we've grown up and we've realised that we are really brothers. I love yiz and I wish yiz the best in the future whatever happens to all of us. And eh, please God we'll stay friends for a long time.

BP: Give us a little Ro verbal on the different cats.

RONAN: In the beginning everybody kinda saw **Mick** as the oldest and I was the youngest. And then things started to change and I became the senior man in the band. I guess I was one of the lucky ones in the band, chosen to sing most of the songs and be pushed to the front. But myself and Mick, we've become more friends now than we ever have. He's a very strong minded person, has his own feelings, keeps to himself. We go on to **Shane**. Everyone knows what Shane is like. Shane is the cool, calm, collected person in the band, he just takes everything in his stride and deals with it, doesn't care about too much. Wonderful person, very strong, you can always look for support from Shane. And he loves his cars! (laughs). **Keith** wears his heart on his sleeve. He has the biggest heart in the world. He means a lot to me. Well, all the guys mean a lot to me but Keith and myself and probably Stephen, we've seen each other a lot outside of Boyzone. He's a dear

friend and and he's very very funny too and we always have a good laugh. **Steo** is the very shy one, sits in the back, very quiet, very loving, big-hearted character. Yeah, a very loving man is Steo. All the lads, we've opened our hearts to each other, the five of us, which nobody else would see. But it's wonderful, it's like a kinship, a brotherhood, you know? It's a time, a chapter in our book, that we all hold very special to ourselves and we've also learned an awful lot from each other. But, my God, it's been an incredible ride, a wonderful ride. I love those guys with all my heart.

BP: Okay, final words to the world....

RONAN: To everyone, to the fans, to the guys, to the families of the guys, to everybody who's been a part of Boyzone for the last six years.... thank you. You know that without everyone of you we would not be here today. To the mothers of Keith, Shane, Stephen and Mikey, without them we wouldn't be what we are today. And to my Mam for giving me .... just for giving me the space and the opportunity to do this and respecting me and being there for me and letting me go when I had to go. I miss you Mam, thank you.

BP: God bless you, Ro. Long may you boogaloo, baby.

RONAN: God bless yiz all and I want to thank the other five guys again for the love and respect they've shown me over the years.

BP: Four guys.

RONAN: Other four guys, sorry. Well Him upstairs too. That's number five (laughs).

BP: Keep on rockin' in the free world (laughter).

THANX
VIBRATIONAL VIBRAPHONIC VIBES
My godson Danny Dennehy.
Patricia Fallon.
Sinéad O'Connor.
Annette Tallon.
Patsy & Martha. Rachel & Jenny & Sarah.
Barney & Hedge & Billy.
Gerry O'Boyle & all @ Filthy
   McNasty's, London.
Phillip Dodd. Kirsty MacColl.
John Sutton.
Henry McCullough & Josie. Eddie Rowley &
   Gavin McClelland.
Annie, Isabel & Luci of Chicks.
Jimmy & Robert. Ian Dury.
Keef & Ronnie. Fatboy Slim &
The Chemical Brothers.
Bono & David Bowie. Fiachna & Suki.
James Wright. Brian Adams & Jedda Downey.
Business Affairs: Alan Duffy @
   OJ Kilkenny & Co, Dublin.
Legal Affairs: James O'Malley @
   James O'Malley & Co. NYC.
Simon Kenton & Helen Ledger @ Idols.
Adele Ryder @ Shoot.
Candida Bottaci @ Principle Management.
Caroline McAteer & The Outside
   Organisation.
Allison Maund & Boyzone Magazine.
Miranda Sale & Georgie Manners @ CPL.
To all the photographers, especially
   Sinéad & Stephen, Ray & Philip.
BP's prints: Declan 'Barney' Barnes @
   Kevin Dunne's Studio, Neasa De Cleir.
Transcription & Typing: Eugene Archer
   & Suzanne Kavanagh.
Lucian Grainge, David Joseph, Jason Iley,
   Colin Barlow, Orla Quirke, Cynthia Lole,
   Celina Webb, Annabelle Scott Curry &
   all @ Polydor.
Clare Hulton, Charlotte Glover,
   Guillaume Mussaars & all @ Boxtree.
Art Direction by Steve Averill &
   Design by Siobhan O'Carroll
   @ Averill Brophy Associates-Dublin.
Yvonne Keating & Lisa Duffy. Jack & Jordon.
Mark Plunkett & Barrie Knight.
Louis Walsh & John Reynolds, Carol Hanna,
   Lorraine Kinahan & Clare Byrne
   @ War Management.
Ronan Keating, Stephen Gately, Keith Duffy,
   Shane Lynch & Mikey Graham.
You.
Me.
Serendipity.
"Nothing you can do that can't be done"
   -John Lennon.

   -BP FALLON, Dublin 1999